I0012290

C++ Programming Language Guide for Experts

Understanding the Benefits of C++ Programming Language

By

Aden Fraser

Table of Contents

CHAPTER 1

Introduction

1.1 What is C++ Programming Language

C++ is a versatile and powerful programming language that has been a cornerstone of software development for several decades. It was developed as an extension of the C programming language, with the "++" symbolizing the incremental improvements and additions made to C. C++ was created by Bjarne Stroustrup in the early 1980s at Bell Labs and has since become one of the most widely used programming languages in the world.

C++ is known for its combination of high-level and low-level programming features, making it suitable for a wide range of applications, from system-level programming to building complex software systems. It is classified as a multi-paradigm language, which means it supports various programming styles, including procedural, object-oriented, and generic programming. This versatility makes C++ an attractive choice for both beginners and seasoned developers.

One of the key features of C++ is its focus on efficiency and performance. It provides direct access to memory and hardware resources, allowing developers to write code that executes quickly and efficiently. This level of control over system resources is essential for tasks such as game development, system software, and embedded systems programming.

C++ also places a strong emphasis on code reusability and modularity. Object-oriented programming (OOP) concepts, such as classes and inheritance, allow developers to create reusable code components, making it easier to build and maintain large software projects. Furthermore, C++ supports the Standard Template Library (STL), which provides a collection of data structures and algorithms that can be used out of the box, saving developers time and effort in implementing common functionalities.

1.2 Benefits of C++ Programming Language

C++ offers a wide array of benefits that have contributed to its enduring popularity in the world of programming:

1. **Performance**: C++ allows for low-level memory manipulation and direct access to hardware, resulting in highly efficient code execution. This is crucial for applications like video games, real-time simulations, and system-level programming.

2. **Versatility**: C++ supports multiple programming paradigms, including procedural, object-oriented, and generic programming. Developers can choose the style that best suits their project's needs.

3. **Reusability**: Object-oriented features in C++, such as classes and inheritance, promote code reusability and maintainability. This leads to shorter development cycles and reduced maintenance efforts.

4. **STL**: The Standard Template Library (STL) in C++ provides a rich set of data structures and algorithms, reducing the need to reinvent the wheel and accelerating development.

5. **Compatibility**: C++ is compatible with C, which means C code can be integrated seamlessly into C++ projects. This is advantageous when working with legacy code or libraries.

6. **Strong Community and Resources**: C++ has a vast and

active developer community, offering access to tutorials, forums, libraries, and tools. This support network makes it easier to learn and master the language.

7. **Cross-Platform Development**: C++ can be used to develop applications for various platforms, including Windows, macOS, Linux, and embedded systems, making it suitable for a wide range of projects.

8. **Ecosystem**: C++ has a rich ecosystem of development tools, including integrated development environments (IDEs), compilers, and debugging tools, making it well-suited for professional software development.

C++ is a versatile and powerful programming language with a rich history and a wide range of applications. Its performance, flexibility, and extensive ecosystem make it a valuable tool for both beginners and experts in the field of software development. Whether you're building high-performance applications or tackling complex programming challenges, C++ remains a language of choice for many developers around the world.

CHAPTER 2

Advanced C++ Concepts

2.1 Templates and Generic Programming

Templates in C++ allow you to write generic code that can work with different data types without having to rewrite the same code for each type. This is known as generic programming. Templates enable you to create functions and classes that can adapt to various data types, making your code more flexible and reusable. They are particularly useful when you want to create data structures or algorithms that work with different data types but follow a similar logic.

2.2 Smart Pointers and Memory Management

Smart pointers are a modern C++ feature that helps manage memory more effectively than traditional raw pointers. They automatically handle the allocation and deallocation of memory, helping to prevent memory leaks and issues like "dangling pointers." Smart pointers come in several flavors, such as **std::shared_ptr**, **std::unique_ptr**, and **std::weak_ptr**, each serving specific memory management needs. They make your code safer and more robust by providing automatic memory cleanup when objects are no longer needed.

2.3 Exception Handling Strategies

Exception handling in C++ allows you to deal with errors and exceptional conditions gracefully. It involves throwing and catching exceptions to handle runtime errors without crashing the program. Exception handling strategies include using **try**, **catch**, and **throw** keywords. By employing exception handling effectively, you can separate error-handling logic from the normal flow of your program, making it more robust and maintainable.

2.4 Operator Overloading and Custom Operators

C++ allows you to redefine the behavior of operators for user-defined types through operator overloading. This means you can create custom implementations for operators like +, -, *, /, and more, so they work with your custom classes and objects. Operator overloading makes your code more intuitive and expressive, enabling you to write code that reads like natural language when working with user-defined types.

2.5 RAII (Resource Acquisition Is Initialization)

RAII is an important C++ programming concept that ties resource management to object lifetime. The idea is that when you acquire a resource (like memory, file handles, or network connections), you should associate it with an object. When that object goes out of scope (i.e., is destroyed), the resource is automatically released. This ensures that resources are properly cleaned up and prevents resource leaks. RAII is commonly used with smart pointers and is a fundamental technique for writing safe and resource-efficient C++ code.

These advanced C++ concepts are essential for mastering the language and writing efficient, maintainable, and error-resistant code.

Understanding these concepts will enable you to leverage the full power of C++ in your software development projects.

CHAPTER 3

Advanced Object-Oriented Programming

3.1 Inheritance and Polymorphism

Inheritance is a fundamental concept in object-oriented programming (OOP) that allows you to create new classes (derived or child classes) by inheriting properties and behaviors from existing classes (base or parent classes). In C++, inheritance is implemented using the **class** or **struct** keyword, followed by a colon and the base class name. Inheritance facilitates code reuse and promotes the creation of hierarchies of related classes.

Polymorphism is a key OOP concept that enables objects of different classes to be treated as objects of a common base class. This allows you to write code that can work with objects of various derived classes in a generic way. Polymorphism in C++ is achieved through function overriding and virtual functions. Virtual functions are functions in the base class that can be overridden by derived classes, ensuring that the correct method is called at runtime based on the actual object type.

Polymorphism comes in two forms:

- **Compile-time (Static) Polymorphism:** This is achieved

through function overloading and operator overloading. It allows you to select the appropriate function or operator at compile time based on the function's signature or the operator being used.

- **Runtime (Dynamic) Polymorphism:** This is achieved through virtual functions and function overriding. It allows the selection of the appropriate function at runtime based on the actual object's type.

Polymorphism enhances code flexibility and extensibility by allowing you to create more generic and reusable code that can work with a variety of derived classes without the need for explicit type checking.

3.2 Abstract Classes and Interfaces

Abstract classes in C++ are classes that cannot be instantiated on their own; they are meant to serve as base classes for other classes. Abstract classes often contain one or more pure virtual functions, which are declared with the **virtual** keyword and no function body. These functions act as placeholders for functionality that derived classes must implement. Abstract classes are used to define a common interface for a group of related classes, ensuring that certain methods are available in all derived classes.

Interfaces in C++ are similar to abstract classes but contain only pure virtual functions. They define a contract that derived classes must adhere to by providing concrete implementations for all the functions declared in the interface. In C++, interfaces are often used to define a common set of methods that multiple unrelated classes need to implement to ensure a consistent interface across different classes.

Both abstract classes and interfaces help enforce a level of structure and consistency in your code by ensuring that derived classes implement specific methods or behaviors. They are crucial for designing extensible and maintainable object-oriented systems and facilitating code collaboration among multiple developers.

Understanding and effectively using these advanced object-oriented programming concepts in C++ can greatly enhance your ability to design and build complex software systems while promoting code reusability and maintainability.

3.3 Multiple Inheritance and Virtual Inheritance

Multiple Inheritance is a feature in C++ that allows a class to inherit properties and behaviors from more than one base class. This means that a derived class can have multiple parent classes. While this feature can be powerful, it can also lead to complex relationships between classes, known as the "diamond problem." In the diamond problem, if a class inherits from two classes that have a common base class, it can result in ambiguity regarding which base class's members should be used. C++ provides mechanisms like virtual inheritance to address this issue.

Virtual Inheritance is a technique used to prevent ambiguity in cases of multiple inheritance. When a class inherits virtually from a base class, it ensures that only a single instance of the base class is included in the inheritance hierarchy, even if multiple paths lead to it. This resolves the ambiguity problem by making sure that there is no duplicated base class when dealing with multiple inheritance scenarios.

3.4 Type Casting and RTTI (Run-Time Type Information)

Type Casting in C++ refers to the conversion of one data type to another. C++ provides several casting operators, such as **static_cast**, **dynamic_cast**, **const_cast**, and **reinterpret_cast**. These operators allow you to change the type of an object or pointer during compilation or runtime, depending on the specific requirements of your code.

- **static_cast** is used for standard type conversions and should be used when you are certain about the types involved.

- **dynamic_cast** is primarily used in situations involving polymorphism, such as casting from a base class pointer to a derived class pointer. It checks at runtime if the conversion is valid.

- **const_cast** is used to add or remove the **const** qualifier from a variable.

- **reinterpret_cast** is used for low-level casting between unrelated types, such as converting a pointer to an integer.

Run-Time Type Information (RTTI) is a C++ feature that provides information about the type of an object during runtime. RTTI allows you to query an object's type and perform dynamic type checking. C++ offers two primary RTTI mechanisms:

- **typeid** operator: Used to obtain information about an object's type. It returns a **type_info** object that can be compared to other **type_info** objects to determine the object's actual type.

- **dynamic_cast** (mentioned earlier) also performs type checking at runtime and is commonly used in combination with polymorphism to ensure safe type conversions.

Understanding multiple inheritance, virtual inheritance, type casting, and RTTI is crucial when working with complex class hierarchies, polymorphism, and situations where you need to manipulate objects of various types dynamically. These concepts enable you to write more flexible and adaptable code, especially in large-scale C++ projects.

CHAPTER 4

Advanced Standard Library Features

4.1 STL Containers and Algorithms

The Standard Template Library (STL) in C++ provides a rich set of containers and algorithms that simplify common programming tasks. **STL Containers** are data structures that store and manage collections of objects. They come in various types, including vectors, lists, sets, maps, queues, and stacks. Each container type has unique characteristics, such as fast random access for vectors, fast insertion/removal for lists, and associative lookups for sets and maps.

STL Algorithms are a set of functions that operate on STL containers and provide operations like sorting, searching, and data manipulation. Examples include **std::sort**, **std::find**, **std::transform**, and many more. These algorithms are generic, meaning they work with different container types, making your code more generic and reusable.

4.2 Advanced STL Features (e.g., Allocators)

While containers and algorithms are the most commonly used features of the STL, there are more advanced features, such as **Allocators**, that allow you to have fine-grained control over memory allocation and deallocation within containers.

Allocators enable you to customize how memory is managed by STL containers, which can be particularly useful in scenarios where you need to optimize memory usage, integrate with external memory management systems, or work in resource-constrained environments.

4.3 Custom Allocators

Custom Allocators take the concept of allocators a step further by allowing you to define your own memory allocation strategies for STL containers. This can be beneficial in situations where you have specific memory requirements, such as using memory pools, custom memory managers, or allocating memory from non-standard sources. By creating custom allocators, you can tailor the memory management behavior of STL containers to meet the needs of your application.

Understanding these advanced features of the STL is essential for advanced C++ programming, especially when you need to optimize performance, memory usage, or integrate C++ code with other systems. These features give you the ability to fine-tune your code to achieve specific goals and make the most of the powerful tools provided by the C++ STL.

4.4 STL Iterators and Iterator Adapters

STL Iterators are objects that allow you to traverse and manipulate the elements of STL containers. They provide a common interface for accessing elements regardless of the container type. Iterators come in various types, including input iterators, output iterators, forward iterators, bidirectional iterators, and random access iterators, each offering different levels of functionality and efficiency.

- **Input iterators** allow you to read elements from a container sequentially.

- **Output iterators** allow you to write elements to a container sequentially.

- **Forward iterators** offer read and write access, but only in a forward direction.

- **Bidirectional iterators** allow bidirectional movement

(forward and backward) within a container.

- **Random access iterators** provide efficient random access and arithmetic operations (e.g., addition and subtraction).

STL Iterator Adapters are special iterator types that modify or adapt the behavior of existing iterators to suit specific needs. Examples include **std::back_inserter**, **std::front_inserter**, and **std::inserter**, which adapt iterators to insert elements at the back, front, or a specified position of a container, respectively.

4.5 Functors and Lambda Expressions

Functors, short for function objects, are objects in C++ that act like functions. They are instances of classes that define the **operator()** method, which allows them to be called like functions. Functors are often used as arguments to STL algorithms and provide a way to customize the behavior of these algorithms.

Lambda Expressions are a more recent addition to C++ and offer a concise way to create anonymous function objects (functors) inline. Lambda expressions are defined using the **[]** syntax and can capture variables from their surrounding scope, allowing for convenient, localized customizations of behavior within a small code block.

Lambdas and functors are powerful tools for customizing the behavior of algorithms or providing callback functions. They are frequently used to sort, filter, or transform elements in containers based on specific criteria, making code more expressive and readable.

Understanding iterators, iterator adapters, functors, and lambda expressions is crucial for effective use of the C++ Standard Library, as they enable you to work with containers, customize algorithm behavior, and write more concise and expressive code.

CHAPTER 5

Concurrency and Multithreading

5.1 Thread Management and Synchronization

Concurrency in C++ involves managing and coordinating multiple threads of execution to achieve parallelism and efficient resource utilization. Thread management encompasses creating, controlling, and synchronizing threads within a program.

- **Thread Creation**: C++ provides mechanisms to create threads, such as the **std::thread** class. You can spawn multiple threads to perform tasks concurrently, which can lead to improved performance in multi-core systems.

- **Thread Control**: You can manage the lifecycle of threads using functions like **std::thread::join()** or **std::thread::detach()**. Joining a thread means waiting for it to finish its execution, while detaching allows it to run independently.

- **Thread Synchronization**: When multiple threads access shared resources concurrently, synchronization is essential to prevent data races and ensure data integrity. Synchronization mechanisms like mutexes, condition variables, and barriers are used to coordinate thread activities.

5.2 Mutexes and Locks

Mutexes (short for mutual exclusion) are synchronization primitives in C++ used to protect critical sections of code from being executed simultaneously by multiple threads. Mutexes ensure that only one thread can access a shared resource at any given time.

- **Locks**: Locks are used in conjunction with mutexes to acquire and release ownership of the mutex. C++ provides different types of locks, including **std::unique_lock**, **std::lock_guard**, and **std::scoped_lock**, each with specific characteristics and use cases.

- **std::unique_lock** allows more flexibility by enabling deferred locking and timed locking, in addition to standard locking.

- **std::lock_guard** is a simple RAII (Resource Acquisition Is Initialization) lock that automatically unlocks the mutex when it goes out of scope.

- **std::scoped_lock** is used to lock multiple mutexes simultaneously, ensuring that no deadlock can occur due to the order in which locks are acquired.

Mutexes and locks play a crucial role in ensuring thread safety and avoiding race conditions. They help in designing concurrent applications that execute correctly and consistently, even when multiple threads are involved.

Understanding thread management, synchronization, mutexes, and locks is essential for developing robust and efficient multithreaded C++ applications, particularly in scenarios where you need to harness the full potential of modern hardware with multiple cores and processors.

5.3 Atomic Operations and Memory Ordering

Atomic Operations are operations that are performed as a single, indivisible unit, without being interrupted by other threads. In C++, the **<atomic>** library provides a set of types and functions for performing atomic operations on variables, ensuring that multiple threads can safely manipulate shared data without causing data races.

Memory Ordering is the way in which the C++ memory model defines how reads and writes to memory by different threads are ordered or synchronized. Memory ordering ensures that memory operations appear to occur in a consistent and predictable order across threads. C++ provides memory orderings such as **std::memory_order_relaxed**, **std::memory_order_acquire**, **std::memory_order_release**, and others to control how memory accesses are ordered and synchronized between threads.

Using atomic operations and memory orderings is crucial when dealing with shared variables that are accessed and modified by multiple threads simultaneously. These mechanisms ensure that data consistency is maintained and that the behavior of multithreaded programs is well-defined.

5.4 Thread Pools and Asynchronous Programming

Thread Pools are a design pattern in multithreading where a fixed number of worker threads are created and maintained in a pool. Tasks or jobs are submitted to the thread pool, and the available worker threads execute these tasks asynchronously. Thread pools are efficient for managing the overhead of thread creation and destruction, especially in scenarios where tasks are short-lived and numerous.

Asynchronous Programming in C++ involves executing tasks concurrently without explicitly managing threads. C++11 introduced the **<future>** and **<async>** libraries, which allow you to perform asynchronous tasks using **std::async**, **std::future**, and **std::promise** to create and manage asynchronous operations. Asynchronous programming is useful for improving application responsiveness, especially in I/O-bound or parallelizable workloads.

By using thread pools and asynchronous programming, you can harness the power of parallelism and concurrency in C++ while abstracting away some of the complexities of low-level thread management. These techniques are valuable for developing scalable and responsive applications that can efficiently utilize multiple CPU cores and handle concurrent workloads.

CHAPTER 6

Performance Optimization

6.1 Profiling and Benchmarking

Profiling is the process of analyzing a program's runtime behavior to identify performance bottlenecks and areas where optimization is needed. Profiling tools, such as **gprof**, **Valgrind**, or built-in profilers in integrated development environments (IDEs), provide insights into a program's execution time, memory usage, and function call hierarchy.

Benchmarking involves measuring the performance of code or algorithms against specific criteria or competitors. It helps you compare different implementations and determine which one is faster, more memory-efficient, or otherwise better suited to your requirements. Benchmarking can be done using dedicated benchmarking libraries or by writing custom benchmarking code.

To optimize your code effectively, start by profiling it to identify performance hotspots. Once you have identified bottlenecks, use benchmarking to compare different optimizations and choose the most effective approach.

6.2 Optimizing Code for Speed and Memory

Optimizing code for speed and memory efficiency is essential for achieving high-performance C++ applications. Here are some general optimization techniques:

- **Algorithmic Optimization**: Choose the right algorithms and data structures for your problem. Some algorithms have better time complexity or memory usage characteristics than others for specific tasks. Consider algorithmic improvements first.

- **Minimize Memory Allocations**: Memory allocation and deallocation can be expensive operations. Use techniques like object pooling, reuse memory whenever possible, and minimize dynamic memory allocation, especially in tight loops.

- **Cache Optimization**: Optimize your code to take advantage of CPU caches. Accessing data from caches is significantly faster than accessing data from main memory. Keep data locality in mind to reduce cache misses.

- **Inline Functions**: Mark small and frequently used functions as **inline**. This hints to the compiler to replace function calls with the actual code, which can reduce the overhead of function calls.

- **Compiler Optimizations**: Modern C++ compilers perform various optimizations automatically. Use compiler-specific flags (e.g., **-O2, -O3** in GCC) to enable optimization levels. Compiler optimizations can include loop unrolling, instruction reordering, and more.

- **Parallelism**: Take advantage of parallelism, either through multithreading or SIMD (Single Instruction, Multiple Data) instructions. Utilize libraries like OpenMP or Intel Threading Building Blocks (TBB) for multithreaded applications.

- **Profile-Guided Optimization (PGO)**: PGO involves profiling your code with typical input data to guide the compiler in optimizing frequently used paths in your program.

- **Reduce Branching**: Minimize conditional branching in your code, as it can disrupt pipeline execution and lead to

unpredictable performance.
Consider using branch prediction-
friendly constructs.

- **Use Efficient Data Types**: Choose
  the appropriate data types to
  minimize memory usage. For
  example, use **int** instead of **long** if
  smaller integers are sufficient.

- **Avoid Global Variables**:
  Excessive use of global variables
  can hurt cache coherency and
  make optimization more
  challenging. Prefer passing
  variables as function parameters or
  encapsulating them in classes.

Optimization should be a measured
process. First, profile your code to
identify bottlenecks, then optimize the
most critical parts of your application.
Keep in mind that optimization may
involve trade-offs, such as increased

code complexity or decreased code readability. Balancing performance with maintainability is crucial.

6.3 Cache Optimization Techniques

Optimizing for CPU cache is crucial for improving the performance of your C++ code, as memory access times can be a significant bottleneck. Here are some cache optimization techniques:

- **Data Locality**: Arrange data structures and access patterns to improve data locality. When you access data that is stored close together in memory, it's more likely to be in the CPU cache, resulting in faster access times.

- **Cache-Friendly Data Structures**: Use data structures that are cache-friendly, such as arrays or contiguous memory blocks, to minimize cache misses. This is particularly important for large data sets accessed in tight loops.

- **Loop Unrolling**: Manually unrolling loops can help reduce loop overhead and improve data locality. However, be cautious, as excessive unrolling can lead to code bloat.

- **Data Alignment**: Align data structures and data members to the cache line size. Misaligned data can result in performance penalties due to extra memory fetches.

- **Prefetching**: Use hardware prefetching hints or software prefetching to load data into the cache before it's needed. This can reduce cache miss latency.

- **Cache Blocking**: Divide large data sets into smaller blocks that fit in the cache. Process each block independently to maximize cache usage.

- **Cache-Aware Algorithms**: Design algorithms that take cache behavior into account. For example, consider the cache complexity of sorting algorithms when dealing with large arrays.

- **Minimize False Sharing**: Avoid multiple threads accessing adjacent memory locations simultaneously (false sharing), as it can lead to cache contention. Use padding or alignment to separate data accessed by different threads.

6.4 Inline Functions and Compiler Optimizations

Inline Functions:

- **Inline Functions**: Marking a function as **inline** suggests to the compiler that it should replace function calls with the actual code of the function. This can eliminate the overhead of function call and return instructions, resulting in performance improvements, especially for small and frequently used functions.

- **Discretionary**: The **inline** keyword is discretionary, meaning the compiler may choose to ignore it. Modern compilers use heuristics to decide whether to inline a function based on factors such as the function's size and complexity. You can manually request inlining using compiler-specific attributes or pragmas if needed.

Compiler Optimizations:

- **Compiler Flags**: Use compiler-specific optimization flags (e.g., **-O2**, **-O3** in GCC) to enable various levels of optimization. These flags instruct the compiler to apply a range of optimizations, including loop unrolling, instruction scheduling, and more.

- **Profile-Guided Optimization (PGO)**: PGO is a technique where you first profile your code with typical input data to gather information about the most frequently executed code paths. Then, you recompile your code with the profiling data, allowing the compiler to optimize the hotspots more effectively.

- **Link-Time Optimization (LTO)**: LTO involves performing optimization across multiple translation units during the linking phase. This can lead to more aggressive optimizations that are not possible within individual translation units.

- **Vectorization**: Enable compiler optimizations for vectorization, which uses SIMD (Single Instruction, Multiple Data) instructions to process multiple data elements in parallel. This is especially useful for numerical computations.

- **Function Inlining**: As mentioned earlier, compilers automatically inline small functions, but you can guide the compiler's decisions using attributes or pragmas.

- **Dead Code Elimination**: Modern compilers can eliminate code that is unreachable or does not affect program output. Ensure your code is well-structured and does not contain dead code.

- **Constant Propagation and Folding**: Compilers can replace constant expressions with their computed values, reducing runtime calculations.

Using inline functions and leveraging compiler optimizations can significantly boost the performance of your C++ code. However, it's important to profile and benchmark your code to ensure that the optimizations you apply have the desired impact and do not introduce unexpected behavior or bugs.

CHAPTER 7
Advanced Topics

7.1 Metaprogramming and Template Metaprogramming (TMP)

Metaprogramming in C++ involves writing code that generates or manipulates code at compile-time. It allows you to perform computations, make decisions, and create code structures before your program is actually executed. **Template**

Metaprogramming (TMP) is a specific form of metaprogramming that uses C++ templates to achieve these compile-time computations.

In TMP, you use templates and template specialization to perform operations on types and values during the compilation phase. Common applications of TMP include creating type traits (e.g., determining if a type is an integer), generating code based on type information, and implementing compile-time algorithms.

TMP can be quite complex and challenging, but it's a powerful technique that allows you to write highly efficient and flexible code. It's commonly used in libraries like the Standard Template Library (STL) and Boost to achieve generic and efficient solutions.

7.2 C++17, C++20, and Beyond

C++ is an evolving language, and new standards are periodically released with new features, improvements, and optimizations. Here's a brief overview of C++17, C++20, and what may come beyond:

- **C++17**: C++17 introduced a range of features and improvements, including structured bindings, if constexpr, fold expressions, and various library enhancements. It aimed to simplify code and provide more expressive and safer programming constructs.

- **C++20**: C++20 brought even more significant changes, such as concepts (which allow you to define type requirements on templates), ranges (which provide a more intuitive way to work with sequences), and coroutines (which enable asynchronous and generator-style programming). It also introduced various library enhancements, including more standardized support for threading.

- **C++23 and Beyond**: The C++ Standard Committee continues to work on new standards. Future versions of C++ are expected to include features like reflection (introspection of code at runtime), improvements to metaprogramming, and further library enhancements. The focus remains on making

the language more expressive,
efficient, and safe.

Keeping up with the latest C++ standards and features is essential for staying at the forefront of C++ development. Each new standard brings tools and capabilities that can simplify code, improve performance, and make your programming tasks more efficient.

However, it's important to note that adopting new standards may take time, as compiler support and migration of existing codebases can be non-trivial. Nevertheless, staying informed about the evolving C++ standards can help you make informed decisions about when and how to adopt new features in your projects.

7.3 Design Patterns in C++

Design Patterns are recurring solutions to common software design problems. They provide proven approaches to solving specific challenges in a structured and reusable way. C++ is a language that lends itself well to design patterns due to its support for object-oriented programming (OOP) and generic programming.

Some commonly used design patterns in C++ include:

- **Singleton Pattern**: Ensures a class has only one instance and provides a global point of access to it.

- **Factory Method Pattern**: Defines an interface for creating an object but allows subclasses to alter the type of objects that will be created.

- **Abstract Factory Pattern**: Provides an interface for creating families of related or dependent objects without specifying their concrete classes.

- **Builder Pattern**: Separates the construction of a complex object from its representation, allowing the same construction process to create different representations.

- **Decorator Pattern**: Attaches additional responsibilities to an object dynamically, extending its functionality without altering its class.

- **Observer Pattern**: Defines a one-to-many dependency between objects so that when one object changes state, all its dependents are notified and updated automatically.

- **Strategy Pattern**: Defines a family of algorithms, encapsulates each one, and makes them interchangeable. It lets the algorithm vary independently from clients that use it.

- **Command Pattern**: Encapsulates a request as an object, thereby allowing for parameterization of clients with queues, requests, and operations.

- **Adapter Pattern**: Allows the interface of an existing class to be used as another interface. It is often used to make existing classes work with others without modifying their source code.

Understanding and applying design patterns in C++ can lead to more maintainable, flexible, and extensible software. It promotes best practices in software architecture and encourages reusability and separation of concerns.

7.4 C++ Best Practices for Experts

C++ experts follow a set of best practices to write efficient, maintainable, and reliable code. Some of these best practices include:

- **Use the Latest Standard**: Stay up to date with the latest C++ standards (e.g., C++17, C++20) and leverage their features to write modern and expressive code.

- **Choose the Right Data Structures**: Select appropriate data structures for your specific needs, considering factors like time and space complexity.

- **Memory Management**: Prefer smart pointers and RAII for memory management to avoid resource leaks. Use custom allocators when necessary.

- **Optimize for Performance**: Profile and benchmark your code to identify bottlenecks, and optimize accordingly. Use compiler-specific flags for optimization.

- **Thread Safety**: Pay attention to thread safety in concurrent code. Use mutexes, locks, and atomic operations where needed. Consider lock-free data structures and algorithms.

- **Exception Safety**: Write exception-safe code, ensuring that resources are properly managed and no memory is leaked in the presence of exceptions.

- **Code Review**: Conduct thorough code reviews to catch bugs, ensure code quality, and share knowledge among team members.

- **Documentation**: Provide clear and comprehensive

documentation for your code, including comments, Doxygen-style documentation, and user-friendly interface descriptions.

- **Testing**: Implement unit tests and integration tests to verify the correctness of your code. Use testing frameworks like Google Test or Catch.

- **Static Analysis and Code Linters**: Use static analysis tools and code linters to catch potential issues and enforce coding standards.

- **Continuous Integration**: Set up a continuous integration (CI) system to automate build and testing processes, ensuring code quality and consistency.

- **Code Organization**: Organize your code into logical modules and follow naming conventions to improve code readability and maintainability.

- **Version Control**: Use a version control system (e.g., Git) to track changes, collaborate with others, and manage code history.

These best practices are crucial for writing high-quality, production-ready C++ code. They help you avoid common pitfalls, reduce debugging efforts, and ensure that your code is robust and maintainable, even in complex and large-scale projects.

CHAPTER 8

Tools and Resources

8.1 Debugging Tools

Debugging is a critical part of software development. Here are some popular debugging tools for C++:

- **GDB (GNU Debugger)**: GDB is a powerful command-line debugger available on Unix-like systems. It allows you to inspect and manipulate the state of a running program, set breakpoints, and step through code.

- **LLDB**: LLDB is another debugger, primarily used on macOS and some other platforms. It offers a modern and user-friendly interface for debugging C++ programs.

- **Visual Studio Debugger**: If you're using Visual Studio as your IDE, it provides an integrated debugger with a rich set of features for debugging C++ code.

- **Eclipse CDT Debugger**: Eclipse's C/C++ Development Tools (CDT) plugin includes a debugger with features like code stepping, variable inspection, and memory monitoring.

- **Valgrind**: Valgrind is a memory analysis tool that can detect memory leaks, heap errors, and other memory-related issues in C++ programs. It is particularly useful for tracking down elusive memory bugs.

- **AddressSanitizer and MemorySanitizer**: These are compiler-based tools (part of Clang/LLVM) that can find memory issues at runtime, such as buffer overflows and use-after-free errors. They are valuable for catching memory-related bugs early.

- **GDB-Python and LLDB-Python**: These debugger extensions allow you to write custom scripts and extensions for debugging C++ code, automating repetitive tasks or creating custom debugging commands.

8.2 Code Analysis Tools

Code analysis tools help you identify potential issues in your code and ensure compliance with coding standards. Here are some commonly used code analysis tools for C++:

- **Clang Static Analyzer**: Part of Clang/LLVM, this tool performs static analysis of your code to find bugs, such as null pointer dereferences and memory leaks, without running the program.

- **Cppcheck**: An open-source static analysis tool for C and C++ code. It checks for a wide range of issues, including memory leaks, resource management problems, and coding style violations.

- **PVS-Studio**: A commercial static code analyzer for C, C++, C#, and Java. It offers a wide range of checks and can detect issues like null pointer dereferences and buffer overflows.

- **Coverity**: A commercial static analysis tool that scans C and C++ code for defects, security vulnerabilities, and code quality issues.

- **Clang-Tidy**: Part of Clang/LLVM, Clang-Tidy is a linter tool that checks C++ code against a set of coding guidelines and best practices. It can automatically fix some issues.

- **SonarQube**: An open-source platform for continuous

inspection of code quality, including C++ code. It provides static code analysis and reporting.

- **Cpplint**: A tool that enforces the Google C++ Style Guide and checks C++ code for style violations. It is particularly useful for maintaining code consistency.

- **CppDepend**: A commercial tool for code analysis, visualization, and measurement. It provides insights into code quality, dependencies, and architectural issues.

Using these debugging and code analysis tools can help you catch bugs and improve the quality of your C++ code. They are essential for large codebases and collaborative development environments to ensure code consistency and reliability.